HAL•LEONARD
INSTRUMENTAL PLAY-ALONG

AUDIO
ACCESS
INCLUDED

PLAYBACK+
Speed • Pitch • Balance • Loop

T0058870

LATIN HITS

CONTENTS

To access audio visit:
www.halleonard.com/mylibrary

Enter Code
2769-7571-7829-0913

ISBN 978-0-634-04161-7

HAL•LEONARD®
CORPORATION

7777 W. BLUEMOUND RD. P.O. BOX 13819 MILWAUKEE, WI 53213

Visit Hal Leonard Online at
www.halleonard.com

BÉSAME MUCHO
(Kiss Me Much)

ALTO SAX

Music and Spanish Words by CONSUELO VELAZQUEZ
English Words by SUNNY SKYLAR

rit.

DESAFINADO
(Off Key)

ALTO SAX

English Lyric by GENE LEES
Original Text by NEWTON MENDONCA
Music by ANTONIO CARLOS JOBIM

Lyrics

When I try to sing, you say I'm off key.
Why can't you see how much this hurts me?
With your perfect beauty and your perfect pitch,
You're a perfect terror.
When I come around, must you always put me down?

If you say my singing is off key, my love,
You will hurt my feeling, don't you see, my love?
I wish I had an ear like yours, a voice that would behave.
All I have is feeling and the voice God gave.

You insist my music goes against the rules.
Yes, but rules were never made for lovesick fools;
I wrote this little song for you but you don't care.
It's a crooked song, ah, but all my heart is there.

The thing that you would see if you would play your part
Is even is I'm out of tune I have a gentle heart.
I took your picture with my trusty Rolleiflex.
And now all I have developed is a complex.

Possibly in vain, I hope you weaken, oh, my love.
And forget those rigid rules that undermine my dream
Of a life of love and music with someone who'll understand.
That even though I may be out of tune
When I attempt to say how much I love you,
All that matters is the message that I bring, which is:
My dear one, I love you.

GUANTANAMERA

ALTO SAX

Original Lyrics and Music by
JOSE FERNANDEZ DIAZ (JOSEITO FERNANDEZ)
Music adaptation by PETE SEEGER
Lyric adaptation by HECTOR ANGULO,
based on a poem by JOSE MARTI

rit.

LA BAMBA

ALTO SAX

By RITCHIE VALENS

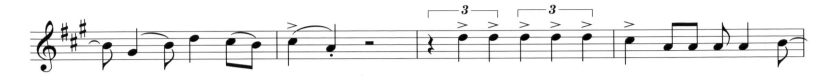

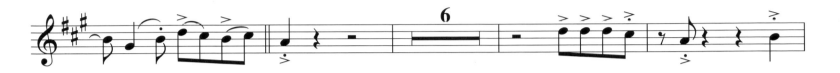

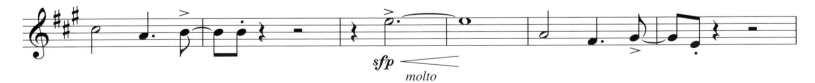

sfp

molto

LLORANDO SE FUE
(La Lambada)

ALTO SAX

Words and Music by ULISES HERMOSA
and GONZALO HERMOSA

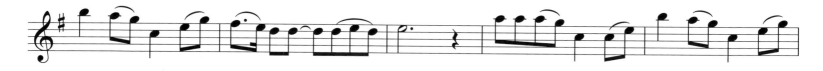

MAMBO NO. 5
(A Little Bit Of...)

ALTO SAX

Words and Music by
DAMASO PEREZ PRADO

MAS QUE NADA

ALTO SAX

Words and Music by JORGE BEN

OYE COMO VA

ALTO SAX

Words and Music by TITO PUENTE

To Coda $\oplus$

D.S. al Coda

$\oplus$ **Coda**

PERHAPS, PERHAPS, PERHAPS
(QUIZAS, QUIZAS, QUIZAS)

ALTO SAX

Music and Spanish Words by OSVALDO FARRES
English Words by JOE DAVIS

19

fpp —————— *mp*

mf

mp

rall.   *p*   *molto rall.*   *pp*

DOS GARDENIAS

ALTO SAX

Words and Music by ISOLINA CARILLO